The Impressionists

Alfred Sisley

Auguste Renoir: Portrait of Alfred Sisley, 1874. Canvas, $25^{1}/_{2} \times 21^{1}/_{4}$ in.
Courtesy of the Art Institute, Mr and Mrs Lewis L. Coburn
Memorial Collection, Chicago.

Alfred Sisley

François Daulte

CASSELL

Contents

Life and works

Documentation

Cassell Publishers Limited
Artillery House, Artillery Row
London SW1P 1RT

© Gruppo Editoriale Fabbri S.p.A., Milan 1972

First published in Great Britain 1988

Translation by Stephen Thorne

British Library Cataloguing in Publication Data

Daulte, François
    Sisley. — The Impressionists.
    1. French paintings. Alfred Sisley
    I. Title   II. Series
    759.4

ISBN 0-304-32222-9

Series edited by Daniel Wildenstein
Produced with the collaboration of the Wildenstein
Foundation, Paris

Photo credits: Durand-Ruel Archives, Paris; François
Daulte Archives, Lausanne; Wildenstein Archives,
New York; Gruppo Editoriale Fabbri, Milan.

Printed in Italy by Gruppo Editoriale Fabbri S.p.A.,
Milan

Why I love Sisley

by Jean-Louis Vaudoyer

**Moret-sur-Loing,
1892.
Pen drawing,
$8^1/2 \times 11^1/2$ in.
Private collection,
Paris.**

The works of Alfred Sisley speak for themselves, but in soft undertones.

Always an Impressionist, he painted only landscapes, and only those of the Ile de France, his own discretion and reserve as a man giving him unique insight into the delicate subtlety of the region's countryside, its charm at once veiled and open to the eye. Of all times of year, Sisley loved best the weeks when winter finally gives way to spring, the weeks of late snows and young buds when nature, not yet fully reawakened, seems to tremble in hesitation before really believing that winter is over at last. These French landscapes yielded all their secrets of rebirth and renewal to Sisley's eye as they had done to Corot's; the work of this Englishman, now become "one of us," seems to bob in the wake of the great Frenchman like the feather of a swan or dove. Sisley's pictures never draw attention to themselves in museums. They wait for you to go to them, to discover for yourself their gentle, murmuring song as simple as it is pure.

Among the brilliant reds of Monet and Pissarro, their glittering rubies, diamonds and emeralds, Sisley shines but never sparkles, like a pearl that, in a certain way, conceals its calmly mysterious irridescence within itself.

Sisley at home

by Gustave Geffroy

Sisley's Cart Pencil drawing, 7$^{1}/_{2}$ × 5 in. Dr. B. Jean Collection.

Together with Théodore Duret and Adolphe Tavernier, Gustave Geffroy was one of the few of the writers and art critics of Sisley's time who established a close friendship with the painter and who knew, loved and understood him well.

I knew Sisley only towards the end of his life. Dinners at which the Impressionists would meet were held every month at the Café Riche, and figures like Claude Monet, Camille Pissarro, Auguste Renoir, Gustave Caillebotte, Dr De Bellio, Théodore Duret, Octave Mirbeau and Stéphane Mallarmé could usually be found at them. Sisley's health was already extremely precarious during the period from 1890 to 1894 when I formed part of their circle, and I had virtually never seen him properly until the day he

asked me to make the easy journey down to Moret, where he was living at the time. I went with Désiré Louis, now dead alas, and the Sisleys—husband, wife and daughter—gave us a wonderful time in their semi-countrified town house right in the centre of the old town. There I got to know my host's painting much better—I had already had the opportunity to admire a group of his works at an exhibition in the Boulevard des Capucines in 1883. Sadly, many of those paintings were still hanging on their creator's walls or were propped up in corners. Sisley was not yet a fashionable painter as Monet was beginning to be, and it was easy enough to discern the sadness that lay behind the resigned exterior and light-hearted words of the melancholy man who was even then making me welcome in his home.

When I look back at that wonderful day made so perfect by Sisley's hospitality and the warmth of the friendship we shared, I always remember feeling that the ageing artist seemed to have fully understood that no ray of fortunate sunshine would ever show the true worth of his paintings to the world in his own lifetime. One reason for this impression is undoubtedly the fact that the people I saw that day have now all passed away, even Sisley's daughter, Jeanne, then in the fulness of her youth and beauty.

Anyway, it was a wonderfully serene and harmonious occasion. After spending the morning in his studio, and then lunch, we all set off in a calèche for Moret, the banks of the Loing and the forest of Fontainebleau, where Sisley treated us to conversation of rare charm and wit. Being an artist and a man of letters, he used exactly the right words when pointing out or explaining things, and I have never since forgotten the splendour of the trees, the open glades and the rocks he commented on in his inimitably poetic way, or his descriptions of the vicissitudes of the river folk whom he knew so well as a result of the years of study and reflection he had passed on the banks of the river under the poplar trees whose leaves still shimmer for us now in his paintings. We parted only towards nightfall, and I didn't see him again until he made another of his increasingly rare trips to Paris. Then, in January 1899, I received a letter from Claude Monet announcing the news of his friend's death: "Poor Sisley asked me to go down and visit him eight days ago, and I realised on that day that he wanted to say farewell to me for the last time. My poor friend, and his poor, poor children."

...Sisley's life was one long struggle, a constant source of worry to him. There was always something that plagued him, he never knew homage or respect from the world. Shortly before his death, he went through those same horrors that attend us when we enter this life. And yet, am I right to say this? We know neither sadness nor desperation when we enter the world, but what bitter melancholy blights the existence of an aged artist who, with a family to support, is obliged nonetheless to come to terms day in and day out with the awful struggle of life and how to get through it. Would it be better to say, then, that this was Sisley's destiny and that he faced it with that fierce, jealously concealed heroism that often ennobles the lives of solitary men in some mysterious way? If he suffered, if he ever despaired, he did it in secret and for those who were dear to him; as far as he himself was concerned, those who knew him throughout his career say that he dedicated himself entirely to his art, which for him was nothing if not his pride in finally getting the better of nature in that struggle that the artist has to enter in to every day that he lives, nothing if not the hope of succeeding in capturing in his paintings something of the fleeting beauty of eternal things. He was not to be betrayed in this hope. The day Sisley's death was announced, after so much suffering endured with a pride that only wished to conceal it from the world, the paintings owned by those who had had faith in his talent suddenly acquired a new value, and all the others scattered around the world, which had been waiting for their true value to be discovered by dealers and for their merits to win the admiration of fickle art enthusiasts, were at once eagerly sought after. Their true worth at last began to be appreciated.

Alfred Sisley has come to occupy his rightful place among the ranks of brilliant landscape painters who have celebrated the beauty of the seasons and the transient charm of the weather and the hours of the day. Any museum or gallery wishing to offer its public a representative account of the great art of the nineteenth-century painters would be failing in its task if it ignored the delicate, softly luminous creations that mark the various stages in the development of Sisley's remarkable talent.

Sisley in *Les Cahiers d'Aujourd'hui*, Editions Crès, Paris, 1923.

Life and works

Training and early works

Road at Marlotte, 1866. Canvas, 19³/4 × 36 in. Albright Knox Gallery, Buffalo (New York).

"A landscape is as full of subtlety and swift changeability as a human face, and to portray on canvas the things of this world, its weather, its eternal substance and the play of light upon it would be a victory indeed for the artist over one of his greatest challenges. An eye for composition and skill in sketching are not enough in themselves to bring about this *resurrection* of the physical appearance of natural phenomena. You have also to be born with a love and understanding of nature, with the gift for getting at the very heart of nature in the things you observe. A vocation can never be forced, and the great landscape painters are as rare as masters in other fields. One such painter was Alfred Sisley." (Geffroy, Sisley, Paris, 1927, pp. 11–12).

In the flowering of French landscape painting that took place towards the end of the nineteenth century, Alfred Sisley more than holds his own with other masters like Monet, Renoir and Cézanne who brought new, vigorous life to the painting of their time. If, on account of the lightness of his palette and his desire to paint in the open air, he is to be counted as one of the first Impressionists, he was able nonetheless to maintain his own independence at all times and to avoid being sucked into a larger group or identified with a trend. The destiny of this painter, English by birth and French by adoption, was strange indeed, for without the slightest deviation from the artistic path he had chosen for himself in life he succeeded in painting some of the most exquisitely restrained and harmoniously executed landscapes ever conceived, his personal tribute to the glorious beauty of the Île de France and the character of the people who live there.

Looking at Sisley's work as a whole, the first thing that strikes us is that it reveals a passionate love of nature almost to the exclusion of anything else. He did, it is true, add a human figure to his paintings here and there, and there are a few rare

still lifes of fruit and game birds, but Sisley was, more than anything else, a painter of landscapes, of the small villages scattered along the banks of the Seine above and below Paris.

Even if he sometimes left his retreat at Louveciennes or, later in life, his beloved house at Moret to go to paint the fogs of London, the regattas at Hampton Court and the cliffs of Langland, he always returned to the small area of France he had chosen for himself. More than the friendship of Monet, Renoir and Bazille, and more than the undeniable charm of Paris, what really counted in Sisley's life were the feelings

1 Auguste Renoir: Portrait of William Sisley the artist's father, 1864. Canvas, 32 × 26 in. Louvre, Paris. (Photo by Routhier)

2 Auguste Renoir: Alfred Sisley and his Wife, 1868. Canvas, 41³/₄ × 29 in. Wallraf-Richartz Museum, Cologne.

3 The Pheasant, 1867-68. Canvas, 21¹/₂ × 15 in. Private collection, New York.

4 Road near the Park of Courances, 1868. Canvas, 15³/₄ × 25¹/₂ in. Private collection, Paris.

3

Sisley's early landscapes, painted in the forest of Fontainebleau, show the influence of the masters of the Barbizon School. The palette is dark—dull browns, greens and blues. The Road near the park of Courances *is characteristic of his early period. Apart from a few bolder touches here and there that seem to anticipate the Impressionism that was to come later, the painting as a whole has a rather thick opulence reminiscent of Diaz and Corot. Sisley also produced a number of rather more conventional paintings featuring fish (Loing pikes with gleaming scales) and game birds hanging on a wall or laid out on a table. The* Pheasant *is probably the most successful of this series of still lifes—his use of very soft tones to bring out the delicate colouring of the bird's finer feathers against the grey of the rest of its plumage is reminiscent of Monet.*

and experiences that tied him to the banks of the Seine and the Loing, whose people, places and things he knew so well. Having chosen a part of the world for himself, he remained faithful to it ever after.

Sisley's gentle, understated vision of nature and, towards the end of his life, a sort of saddened resignation in the face of the injustices of fate, were both factors which directed him towards the

4

production of landscapes rather than studies of the men who inhabit them. A lover of nature and physical reality, Sisley painted both wherever he found them in lowly manifestations of everyday life and things. For this reason, the development of his talent as a painter matches the course of his own destiny as a man very closely, and is intimately

1

related to the events of his own life. Thus, in order to trace the development of Sisley's art and life, and to understand how the one relates to the physical circumstances, long-standing friendships and shifting fortunes of the other, we have to return to the places where he set up his easel and began to paint.

A love of nature and his profound sense of identification with the natural forces and elements acting upon it, both of them aspects of his character that were to lead him to the very heart and essence of the French landscape of the time, were perhaps the result of his English origins and upbringing. Although he

was born in Paris, on 30th October 1839, Sisley was British by parentage. His Mancunian father, William Sisley, ran a business that exported artificial flowers to South America, and his mother, Felicia Sell, was born into an ancient, highly cultured London family from which she acquired her love of music and social life.

As a matter of course, then, Alfred's parents sent him to London at the age of eighteen to learn about business and to prepare himself for a career in commerce and trade. However, instead of busying himself with the problems of the cotton and coffee trade during his

apprentice years in London (1857-1861), the young Sisley spent most of his time visiting museums, and became an enthusiastic admirer of the free-hand sketches of Constable, Bonington and Turner. The works of these English landscape masters almost seems to prefigure his own later development as a painter—the feeling for light, the purity of line, a measured sense of values and, above all, a simple, uncomplicated love that only wishes to show things as they really are, an art which, while firmly believing that it is simply copying things, in fact transforms and transfigures them.

In the spring of 1869, Sisley painted what he saw from the windows of the flat he had rented in 29 Cité-des-Fleurs in the Batignolles. A field of saplings, a winding lane with a few travellers on it, a cart pulled by a white horse and, most importantly, a tranquil horizon and an enormous sky—these things provided more than enough raw material for Sisley to render the rather melancholy

charm of this secluded area in the rural outskirts of Paris. The houses of Montmartre and, on the hilltop, the Moulin de la Galette, can be seen in the background. This part of Paris has now lost the rural appearance it had before the outbreak of the Franco-German War in 1870, when Sisley and his friends used to go there to paint.

1 **Avenue of Chestnuts at La Celle-Saint-Cloud, 1865. Canvas, 49 × 80³/4 in. Musée du Petit-Palais, Paris.**

2 **Montmartre from the Cité-des-Fleurs, 1869. Canvas, 27¹/2 × 46 in. Musée des Beaux-Arts, Grenoble.**

2

We can easily see, then, how the young Sisley found the theories of Charles Gleyre, the historical painter who regarded landscape as a "decadent art," so alien to his talent and aspirations. He was drawn irresistably towards the examples of Constable and Turner, and on returning to Paris in the spring of 1862 obtained his parents' permission to abandon his commercial career and devote himself to his painting.

Thus it was that the young man went in the following October to work in the studio of Gleyre himself, who had suddenly risen to fame after producing his *Evening—Lost Illusions*. There, Sisley was able to meet several other young artists of his own age—the Parisian Auguste Renoir, Claude Monet from Le Havre, and Fédéric Bazille from Montpelier. In spite of their widely differing origins, backgrounds and temperaments, the four young men quickly became inseparable friends. All four would soon play a part in the renascence of French painting that would re-establish the connection between man, nature and light, and which would later come to be known as Impressionism.

For a period of months, Sisley went daily to Gleyre's studio to work with models and to learn how to draw, but he quickly realised that Gleyre's ideas about art were totally opposed to his own and his friends' way of seeing things. Gleyre believed that the landscape was not a worthy subject for a painter.

"In nature," wrote Emile Montégut in *Nos morts contemporains* (2nd series, Paris, 1884, p. 145), "he saw only frames and backgrounds, and in fact he never himself made anything other than a purely accessory use of nature in his own paintings."

Sisley was not prepared to regard landscape painting as a decadent form of art—decadent, that is, in relation to the works of Corot, Rousseau and Courbet. On the contrary, he went on to make the landscape the central feature of his art, seeking to capture every subtlety of its physical appearance. His apprenticeship under Gleyre was destined to be short-lived, then. He left his studio in the spring of 1863 and, taking his friends, future Impressionists all, with him went to paint in the open air on the edge of the forest of Fontainebleau, *sur le motif* as Cézanne would later say.

However, Sisley's origins and his discovery of the English landscape cannot, in themselves, fully account for his reaction to Gleyre's theories of art. If Sisley failed to be influenced by the ideas and tastes of the Swiss painter and, indeed, ended up opposing them, it was because he himself had a deep love of the countryside and powerful yearning for solitude. According to the writer Gustave Geffroy, who knew Sisley well towards the end of his life, the most unpromising of subjects moved Sisley as greatly as the most radiant of human faces; no place was ugly to him because the relationship between earth and sky, and the light and colour of the scene were enough to make it beautiful in his eyes.

After leaving the Académie Gleyre, Sisley rented a flat at 31 Avenue de Neuilly near the Porte Maillot. At

Barges on the Saint-Martin Canal, 1870.
Canvas, $21^{1}/_{2} \times 29$ in.
Oskar Reinhart am
Römerholz Collection,
Winterthur.

that time the outskirts of Paris were still countrified, and the painter had no need to go far from home to find real countryside. He remained in Paris until 1870, dividing his time between studio and open-air work. Later he moved from Avenue de Neuilly to 15 Rue de Moncey, then to 19 Rue de la Paix, and finally to the Cité-des-Fleurs in the Batignolles.

However, as soon as the spring came Sisley would leave Paris to go and paint in the forest of Fontainebleau with Monet, Renoir and Bazille. Sometimes they rented rooms from *père* Paillard at the "Cheval-Blanc" in Chailly-en-Bière, or else stayed in *mère* Anthony's boarding house in Marlotte. It was during one of these excursions in April 1868 that Renoir painted a portrait of Sisley and his young wife, Marie Eugénie Lescouezec from Toul in the Meurthe, who had met Sisley in Paris and married him in 1866. They had two children, Pierre who died a bachelor in 1929, and Jeanne who married Fernand Diets.

Renoir's charming portrait gives us a glimpse of the private life of the young couple. Madame Sisley in her crinoline dress is leaning affectionately on her husband's arm, while he gazes at her tenderly, leaning towards her as if to protect her. As he poses for his friend, Sisley is dressed like a middle-class young man of the period—a light-coloured jacket, grey trousers and top hat. He fully believed in the dignity of his art, and never affected a Bohemian way of life.

When in Paris between his visits to Chailly-en-Bière or Honfleur, Sisley liked to go in the late afternoon to the Café Guerbois at 11 Grand' Rue des Batignolles, five minutes' walk from his studio in the Cité-des-Fleurs, where he would meet the old artists of Gleyre's studio and the Académie Suisse gathered around their master, Edouard Manet, the oldest of them all. Other interesting people went to the Café, critics like Duranty, Philippe Burty and Armand

1

Silvestre, the novelist Emile Zola and his childhood friend Paul Cézanne, the drawer Constantin Guys, the photographer Nadar, and the society painter Alfred Stevens. He would also meet the librettist Blau, and Fioupou, deputy minister at the Ministry of Finance and avid collector of prints, who would recount the lives of artists like Delacroix and Baudelaire who were quite unknown at the time. Sometimes the photographer Carjat, friend of Courbet and Nadar, would suddenly appear, a high-spirited man of some wealth who would amuse the company with his eccentric way of dressing.

Sisley painted little before the war in 1870. Thanks to his father's wealth, he was able to indulge his love for art to the full without having to worry about going places in life. For some years he was fortunate enough to be able to work as an amateur—a *lover* of art, in the strict sense of the term—concerning himself only with making his life better and more beautiful rather than with earning his daily bread.

Sisley's early landscapes painted at La Celle-Saint-Cloud or Marlotte, and especially those sent later to the Salon, are produced with a dark palette of dull browns, greens and blues, and almost all of them have an uncompromisingly severe, flat look about them. After rejecting the tenets of his master Gleyre,

Sisley then sought a compromise that could accomodate both his own instincts and his admiration for Corot and Courbet, whom he acknowledged as his precursors and masters. The two most characteristic paintings of his early period are, perhaps, *The Road at Marlotte*, now in the Albright-Knox Art Gallery, Buffalo, and the *View of Montmartre*, now in the Museum of Grenoble. They are already typical of Sisley's essential style: the flair for composition, the love of space, the carefully studied contrasts of light and shade and, above all else, a sense of the *value* of what is shown.

Unlike Degas and Renoir, Sisley was never attracted by the human face as a subject. He painted several figures in indoor settings, but these pictures could never be described as portraits in the true sense of the term. They are general scenes in which a human figure, caught in a moment of contemplation or while concentrating on some ordinary household task, lends warmth to the setting in which he or she is portrayed. In The Lesson, *Sisley shows us his children, Jeanne and Pierre, busy with their homework. "The light," writes Gustave Geffroy, "plays gently on the white smock of the boy leaning over his book and on the attentively poised head of the girl. There is a sense of silent concentration, one can hear the ticking of the alabaster clock." Wishing, as did also his friends Renoir and Bazille, to paint in the open air in the midst of nature or, as Cézanne would later put it, sur le motif, Sisley often took his easel to the forest of Fontainebleau. In 1869, for example, he painted a country warden crossing a clearing in the forest. This beautiful landscape has many pre-Impressionist elements. Sisley attempted not only to capture the effect of the sunlight filtering down through the tree-tops, but also to give an impression of space by skilfully contrasting the various areas of light and shade.*

1 Country Warden in the Forest of Fontainebleau, 1870. Canvas, $30^3/4 \times 24^3/4$ in.
   Private collection, New York.

2 The Lesson, 1871. Canvas, $15^3/4 \times 18^1/2$ in.
   Private collection, Paris.

2

Towards 1870, however, when he took his easel down to the banks of the Seine and along the Paris canals, Sisley adopted a freer style and a lighter palette. His *Barges on the Saint-Martin Canal* uses Impressionist techniques for the first time in its light shades and carefully calibrated colour arrangements and contrasts. The reflection of the trees in the canal and the rippling of the waves are rendered by splashes of light, small comma-like dabs of colour carefully juxtaposed yet clearly separated. There is more, however. With its dark-hulled barges trimmed in white and the busy group of stevedores on the wharf, Sisley's landscape, now in the Oskar Reinhart collection, seems to anticipate the beautiful series of French canals and rivers he would work on right up to his death.

Then, as a result of the dramatic events of the Franco-German war, Sisley's father began to find his business going downhill. In 1871 he was ruined by a sudden collapse in trade and died soon after. Now left without financial assistance from his family, Sisley discovered virtually over night that the only source of income he had was his painting. In order to support his wife and two children, then, he had to devote himself entirley to the painter's craft.

The Poet of the River Banks

The Seine at Argenteuil, 1872. Canvas, $19^3/4 \times 28^3/4$ in. Private collection, New York.

1

During the period of the Paris Commune, Sisley took refuge with his family in the village of Voisins-Louveciennes, thirty kilometres outside Paris. He rented a small house, 2 Rue de la Princesse, not far from where Renoir and his brother Edmond were living, and with whom he would often go to paint in the forest of Marly, near the acqueduct. It was from this vantage point that Sisley saw Paris burning in the distance on 26th May 1871. Totally powerless, he feared for the safety of the masterpieces in the Louvre, which fortunately were saved. However, other art treasures suffered irreparable damage. In a letter dated 3rd June, his patron Edmond Maître from Bourdeaux gave him an account of the damage: "I don't think there's much point in mentioning the fires and killings—the papers are full of it all already. I mourn above all else the loss of the Hôtel de Ville which contained two real marvels, the ceilings by Ingres and Delacroix, and the fire at the Cour des Comptes that housed the *Justinian*, which has certainly fared no better in the fire in Paris than it did in the fire in Bordeaux".

In 1872, at a time when Paris was

22

2

1 **The Seine at Argenteuil, 1872.**
   Canvas, 18 × 25¹/₂ in.
   Private collection, Lausanne.

2 **The Square at Argenteuil, 1872.**
   Canvas, 18 × 25¹/₂ in. Louvre, Paris.

During his years at Louveciennes, Sisley became, above all else, a painter of the Seine, whose quiet flow and green banks he deeply loved. He was a supreme painter of water, its opaque fluidity and movement in stasis offering him endless opportunities to paint white sails and fishing boats against the larger expanse of the sky. The gentle flow of the French rivers is portrayed for all time in his paintings. Sisley could look at any landscape and skilfully capture its essentials with great economy of means, whether in clouds towering into the sky, or dark-coloured barges outlined in white or vermillion, the plumes of smoke curl-

ing from chimney pots or, sometimes, crowds of people swarming across bridges or along river banks. Sisley's subtlest and most original work was perhaps produced during the period from 1872 to 1874. Like Corot in his Cathedral of Chartres or The Church Tower at Douai, he succeeded in capturing the effect of eternally youthful light on aged stone. The yellow and white façades in the Square at Argenteuil are exactly right, finely drawn with every detail rendered. The shutters, for example, are bright green in the sunlight but blue-grey in the shadows.

Sisley 72

1

2

devoid of intellectual and artistic life, Sisley met Paul Durand-Ruel, whose gallery was inclined to look favourably on young, independent artists. He was introduced to him by Monet and Pissarro, who had become friends of the Paris art dealer during the war while they were staying in London. From then on, Durand-Ruel began to show interest in Sisley's work and to buy his pictures, and would continue to do so for another twenty-five years, to the extent that almost four hundred of Sisley's paintings ended up in his hands. If we bear in mind that, virtually until Sisley's death, it was difficult, if not impossible to sell *any* of his paintings, it is easy to see that Durand-Ruel's purchases, although made at relatively low prices ranging from two to three hundred francs per picture, called for some financial sacrifice on his part and not a little courage.

Sisley's output was abundant throughout the four years he spent at Louveciennes. As soon as the winter was

1 **A District of Louveciennes, 1872. Canvas, 18 × 15³/₄ in. Private collection, Paris.**

2 **The Village on the Edge of the Wood, Autumn Scene, 1872. Canvas, 19³/₄ × 25¹/₂ in. Private collection, Paris.**

over, he would start combing the surrounding countryside for new subjects to paint. He carried his easel to Villeneuve-la-Garenne, to Argenteuil, to the island of the Grande Jatte and to the banks of the Seine near Saint-Denis. However, it is not enough simply to say that Sisley preferred to paint in Louveciennes and its immediate surroundings; it is also important to consider how he *saw* the town and the countryside around it.

First of all, it should be noted that Sisley saw nature in terms of depth rather than in terms of surfaces. Unlike the pure Impressionists such as Monet or Guillaumin, he always maintained that the rendering of space was essential to all painting, the most characteristic element of the art, and that it could not and should not be absent. This is probably why Sisley so often painted tree-lined roads gradually disappearing into the distance. The *motif* of the "perspective" road appears perhaps for the first time

1   The Seine at Point-du-Jour, 14th July 1873. Canvas, 15 × 18 in. Private collection, London.

2   The Seine at Point-du-Jour, 14th July 1873. Pen drawing. Private collection, New York.

3   Photograph of scene painted by Sisley in 1873. (see p. 27).

4   Louveciennes, Rue de Sèvres, 1873. Canvas, $21^{1}/_{2} \times 28^{3}/_{4}$ in. Musée d'Orsay, Paris.

4

In 1873, while on the quayside at Point-du-Jour, Sisley produced first a rough sketch showing the 14th July celebrations, and then later an oil on the same theme. The flags flying in the breeze, the lively crowds on the quayside and the boats gliding over the water are perfectly caught in their essential truth, and the style is now decidedly Impressionist.

Sisley did not hesitate to render the shadows of the leaves with violet blues, and his whole technique is much freer. Sisley was perfectly aware of this development in his work, and explained several years later to the art critic Adolphe Tavernier what he had been trying to do: "Although a landscape painter should always remain in control of what he is doing, the actual execution of

his paintings should also, in certain rather more intense moments, communicate what the painter feels about his subject to the viewer. You will see, then, that I'm in favour of using a range of different techniques in the same painting. This opinion is not widely shared, but I'm convinced I'm right, especially when one is trying to capture a certain effect of the light. The sun softens some parts of a landscape, but it brings others into high relief, and these light effects, which are translated physically into nature itself, should also be rendered physically on the canvas."

A careful examination of The Seine at Point-du-Jour shows what Sisley meant by "range of different techniques." In order to capture the sparkle of the water and

the reflections of objects in it, Sisley covered the foreground of the canvas in small dabs of boldly applied colour, while the trees and sky in the back-ground are almost plain by comparison.

The "perspective" road disappearing into the distance or winding across the canvas were very important in Sisley's work because they allowed him to give free expression to his love of space. Even the small figures that frequent these roads—the Rue de Sèvres or the Village Road at Louveciennes—with their bodies elongated almost as if they had been painted by Jongkind, are not intended to lend life to the scene, but to add perspective reference points in the landscape and to indicate the true proportions of natural objects.

in Hobbema's famous *Avenue in Middle-harnis* which Sisley had been able to examine in the National Gallery in London. Later on, Corot in his *Ruede Sèvres* and Paul-Camille Guignon in his *Rue de Gineste* near Marseilles would also paint tree-lined country roads with travellers returning home to their villages.

The Impressionists, and Renoir and Pissarro in particular, would later take up the theme, but it was Sisley more than any of them who made it really important in his work, who painted the winding road as it entered Louveciennes, or tree-lined roads snaking among the vines and tall grass. His love of space and depth is ever-present in his work. Second, we might note that, in order to paint the special part of France he had chosen, Sisley created a palette that scandalised the public of his day but which now, far from seeming extreme in any way, appears admirably well-balanced and generally restrained in conception. Through his skill in catching the most subtle effects of light without thereby rendering his forms abstract, Sisley also demonstrated his skill as a colourist and his acute powers of observation. Unlike so many other lesser masters of the nineteenth century who painted new subjects without, however, really modifying their way of *seeing* things, Sisley was modern in more than just intention. In his case, the discovery of new subjects was matched by new developments in his technical expertise. Whether in *The Seine at Argenteuil*, the *Rue de Sèvres* or in the bare trees standing stark against the sky at Vaissons, he was able to create effects that are as right as they are original, even though he restricted himself to the use of certain slate blues, salmon pinks and lilacs that only he, of all painters, knew how to produce.

Sisley took part in the First Exhibition of Impressionist Artists (Société anonyme des Artistes Peintres, Sculpteurs, Graveurs) held in the gallery of his photographer friend Nadar at 35

1

1   **Auguste Renoir: Portrait of Paul Durand-Ruel, 1910. Canvas, 32 × 25^1/$_2$ in. Durand-Ruel Collection, Paris.**

2   **Road at Louveciennes, 1874. Canvas, 25^1/$_2$ × 21^1/$_4$ in. Private collection, Paris.**

Born in Paris on 31st October 1831, Paul Durand-Ruel began his career as a cadet officer at the Military College of Saint-Cyr. However, bad health forced him to abandon a military career and he chose instead to become an art dealer. He married Jeanne-Marie-Eva Calon on 4th January 1862 and she later bore him five children: Joseph, Charles, Georges, Marie-Thérèse and Jeanne. Champion and friend of the Impressionists, Durand-Ruel's ceaseless advocacy, courage and artistic intuition did much to bring their work before the public and to consolidate their reputations in both Europe and America. The friendship between Sisley and Durand-Ruel was long-standing and deepened over the years. Durand-Ruel had a magnificent collection of Sisley's pictures and works by other Impressionists in his apartment in Rue de Rome.

1

1   Snow at Louveciennes, 1874. Canvas, $18^1/2 \times 22$ in. Courtauld Institute Galleries, London.

2   Regattas at Molesey, 1874. Canvas, $24^1/2 \times 36$ in. Louvre, Paris.

3   Regattas at Hampton Court, 1874. Canvas, 18×24 in. Private collection, Zurich.

2

Apart from a view of Charing Cross Bridge in which Sisley brilliantly rendered the dark, foggy sky of the British capital using a delicate, pointilliste technique, the landscapes produced during his second visit to Great Britain all depict the River Thames and its tree-lined banks. Sisley's attention was drawn at times to the town of Hampton Court with its iron bridge, shady avenues and peaceful inhabitants out walking or fishing along the river banks, and at others to Sunday scenes of skiffs gliding quickly over the water or small boats with full sails. Sisley rendered these busy scenes of ordinary life in his Regattas at Molesey, formerly part of the original Caillebotte collection and now in the Louvre in Paris. The swiftly-moving skiffs have just set off, the judges are busy about their work in the river meadow and the colours of the flags and banners are reflected on the surface of the river. With its Impressionist technique, light palette and careful rendering of the effects of light on water, Sisley's Regattas should properly be grouped with Monet's Sailing Ships at Chaton and Renoir's Rowers on the Seine painted near Bougival. These paintings also anticipate a number of Caillebotte's later compositions of around 1887 when he had settled at Petit-Genevilliers near Argenteuil.

Boulevard des Capucines in Paris from 15th April to 15th May 1874. He submitted five paintings, including *Road at Saint-Germain* and *Island of Loge*. Unfortunately, the exhibition was not a success. "The public," wrote Paul Durand-Ruel in his *Memoirs*, "flocked to the exhibition, but obviously they were already prejudiced, and regarded these great artists as a bunch of ignorant, conceited fools who were displaying their eccentricities to get themselves noticed. There was a general upsurge of feeling against them in the public mind and an increase in the ridicule they had to suffer, extending to all reaches of society including the studios, the salons and even the theatres, where they were openly derided."

In spite of all his efforts, Paul Durand-Ruel failed to find buyers for the pictures of Sisley and his friends that he himself had shown such faith in. To avoid financial ruin, he was obliged to cut down on his purchases, and for Sisley, who had virtually no means of subsistence apart from Durand-Ruel's monthly contributions, this was a serious blow indeed.

In order to forget his troubles for a while, Sisley had become accustomed to going to Paris in the early evening to the Café de la Nouvelle-Athènes in the Place Pigalle, where all the independent painters and their friends gathered. There he met not only Manet and Degas, who were older than he was, but also young painters like Franc Lamy, Norbert Goeneutte and Frédéric Cordey. He also met the composer Chabrier there, as well as Cabaner the musician and Lestringuez, a civil servant in the Ministry of the Interior steeped in philosophy and the occult sciences.

Shortly after the First Exhibition of Impressionist Artists, Sisley had the good fortune to be invited to London for a few months by the baritone Jean-Baptiste Faure, one of the first collectors of the pictures of Manet, Monet and their circle.

The painter and his patron arrived in July 1874 and spent four months there. Sisley produced some of his freest, freshest and most untrammelled work during this trip to the capital of the British Isles.

On returning from England, Sisley was

3

informed of the difficult circumstances of the Societé anonyme des Artistes, Peintures, Sculpteurs, Graveurs, whose first exhibition at Nadar's gallery had failed to be the success its organisers had assumed it would be. At 3 pm on 17th December, Sisley took his seat at a general meeting of the Societé called by Renoir. Here are the minutes of the meeting.

"M. Renoir was appointed Chairman.

The Bridge at
Hampton Court, 1874.
Canvas, 18 × 24 in.
Wallraf-Richartz Museum,
Cologne.

1   The Bridge at Hampton Court in a photograph of 1866.

2   A Boarding House at Hampton Court, 1874. Canvas, 20 × 27 in.
    Private collection, Zurich.

3   View of the Thames and Charing Cross Bridge, 1874. Canvas, 13 × 18 in. Baron Louis de
    Chollet Collection, Friburg.

3

The minutes of the last meeting were read and approved.

Treasurer's Report. The Treasurer informed the meeting that once all external debts have been paid, the Society's liabilities will amount to 3713 fr. (monies advanced by members of the Society) while cash reserves amount to only 277,99 fr. Each member will therefore have to deposit the sum of 184,50 fr. in order to pay off these internal debts and re-establish the Society's capital fund.

Given this state of affairs, it seems clear that the liquidation of the Society is the only workable solution This was proposed, put to the vote and unanimously approved.

It was decided that members will be reimbursed the sums they have paid to cover second-year membership costs. A liquidation committee was appointed comprising Mess. Bureau, Renoir and Sisley, who will also be responsible for publishing the Society's legal declarations and accounts.

The meeting was adjourned at a quarter to five.

The Standing Chairman,

Renoir."

Marly-le-Roi and Sèvres

14th July at Marly-le-Roi, 1875. Canvas, 21^{1}/$_{4}$ × 28^{3}/$_{4}$ in. Lady Baillie Collection, London.

Shortly after returning from England, Sisley moved from Louveciennes to Marly-le-Roi, but he was dogged by poverty also there. In an attempt to straighten out his financial difficulties, he decided, with Renoir, Monet and Berthe Morisot, to arrange public auctions of their work in the hope of finding art lovers prepared to buy their pictures.

The first auction was held on 24th March 1875 in the Hôtel Drouot and provoked a demonstration of public disapproval of such vehemence that the police had to be called in. In spite of the support of the art critic Théodore Duret, the painter Gustave Caillebotte and the collector Victor Chocquet, who attempted to push up the prices, Sisley's twenty-one pictures realised only 2440 fr., or an average of little more than 100 fr. for each painting. However, two of the paintings were unusually large, and went for 200 fr. each, while *The Thames Embankment at Hampton Court* was sold, remarkably enough, for 300 fr.

The works Sisley had sent to the First Impressionists Exhibition fared little better. In 1878 he exhibited eight important paintings at the Second Exhibition of the Artistes Indépendant in Durand-Ruel's gallery in 11 Rue de le Peletier, but he failed to sell even one of them. The following year (April 1877) he sent seventeen pictures, including a number of masterpieces like *The Woodcutter*, owned by Dr De Bellio,

Only a few paintings of fruit and flowers are to be found among Sisley's works—grapes and nuts on a white table cloth, some apples and knife, a bunch of wild flowers. With their subtle blendings of colours and the harmony of line created by the round table, the table cloth, the spheres of the fruit and the cutlery, Sisley's still lifes anticipate those which Bonnard and Vuillard would produce a good thirty years later.

In her magical Under the Light of 1877, Marie Brac-

quemond has given us a particularly revealing picture of Alfred Sisley and his wife seated at the dining table in their house in Sèvres. The artist skilfully highlights the soft light filtering through the lampshade to pick out the objects on the tabel in a bravura display of bright points of reflected light.

The life we see is simple and peaceful, as if the artist had caught the Sisleys unawares as they lead their ordinary, day-to-day existence.

4

1 Marie Bracuemond, Under the Light (Sisley and his Wife at Sèvres), 1877. Canvas, 27 × 44^{1}/$_{2}$ in.
Maurice Sternberg Collection, Chicago.

2 Still Life: Apples and Grapes, 1876. Canvas, 15^{3}/$_{4}$ × 24 in. Sterling and Francine Clark Art Institute, Williamstown (Mass.).

3 Still Life: Grapes and Nuts, 1876. Canvas, 15 × 22 in. Private collection, New York.

4 First Frost, 1876. Canvas, 18 × 21^{1}/$_{2}$ in. Private collection, New York.

Banks of the Seine at
Bougival, 1876. Canvas,
15 × 21$^{1}/_{2}$ in. Private collection, New York.

Sisley was a great painter of water, but he was not attracted only to summer landscapes; in fact, he often painted
scenes of flooding in winter. In 1872 he had already
painted the flooding on the Île de la Loge and on the road
from Saint-Germain to Port-Marly caused by the breaking of the river banks, and in 1876 he spent most of his
time painting the flooding at Port-Marly, where he had

only to go down to the banks of the Seine not far from
his house at 4 Rue d'Abreuvoir.
While Monet, in his Débâcles, portrayed vast expanses
of flooding and ice to create an effect of desolate grandeur,
Sisley believed that such natural disasters could be portrayed more effectively through their effect on human be-
ings in the places where they live. For example, The Boat

during the Flood, now in the Louvre, has a kind of
serene peacefulness in spite of the tragic subject and a heavy
sky presaging yet more rain.
The reason, perhaps, is that Sisley knows how to convey
the human element in things. It may be that the water
will slowly rise to cover everything, but the artist still brings
out the perfect blend of cream and pink in the walls of

1 Flooding at Port-Marly, 1872. Canvas, 18 × 24 in. Mr and Mrs Paul Mellon Collection.

2 Flooding at Port-Marly, 1876. Canvas, 23¹/₂ × 32 in. Musée d'Orsay, Paris.

3 Flooding at Port-Marly, 1872. Canvas, 19³/₄ × 25¹/₂ in. Private collection, Paris.

4 Flooding at Port-Marly, 1876. Canvas, 19³/₄ × 24 in. Mrs Antonio Santamarina Collection, Buenos Aires.

3

4

the Nicholas house, and points to the arrival of spring in the young buds appearing on the bare branches of the trees. With his wonderfully sensitive eye, Sisley was able to perceive the subtlest harmonies in nature and capture them on canvas.

Sisley gives a characteristically succinct account of his artistic principles in a letter to his friend, the art critic Adolphe Tavernier: "The subject, the motif, must always be simply rendered in a way that is comprehensible to the viewer and captures his attention. By the elimination of superfluous detail, the viewer should be led to share what it was that moved the painter to paint his picture in the first place. There is always, in a painting, something that the painter really loves. This is one of the reasons why Corot and Jongkind are so fascinating. After the subject itself, one of the most interesting qualities of a painting is movement, life itself."

The Bridge at Argenteuil, belonging to Edouard Manet, and *The Machine at Marly*, belonging to the art critic Théodore Duret, to the Third Impressionists Exhibition, but once again he could not find even one buyer for his pictures, and the press, if it mentioned him at all, was disparaging of his work, except for Georges Riviere in "L' Impressioniste" of 14th April, who paid him just homage: "Sisley is exhibiting more pictures this year than last year, but he has not, for that reason, been spreading his talent too thinly. Ten paintings at most are on show. All of then show the same taste, subtlety and feeling of repose: his great landscape, a road after a shower of rain with water dripping from tall trees on to the sodden ground below and puddles reflecting the light of the sky, is charged with a bewitching poetry. Some light, grey skies, some sunny landscapes and a wonderfully harmonious snow scene round off Sisley's contribution to the exhibition."

Sisley was not discouraged, in spite of the silence and almost unanimous disparagement of the critics, and we know that he often turned to music for refuge and solace. As a young man he had gone to the Pasdeloup Concerts, and one piece that had made an indelible impression on him had been the *Scherzo* of Beethoven's *Septet*. "It seems

Sisley found yet more subjects in the countryside around Sèvres. He went to paint at Suresnes, Meudon, Saint-Cloud and Louveciennes in the winter months particularly, attracted by the ethereal, other-wordly effect of the snow. We may well ask whether those of Sisley's works we find most successful are not, in fact, the ones in which the subject seems to correspond most closely to the painter's mild, contemplative nature.

Unlike Renoir, who loved only green countryside and sunny seashores, calling snow nothing less than "nature's leprosy," Sisley liked to paint winter landscapes in which bare trees standing out against the white ground and grey sky epitomise the melancholy desolation of the frozen countryside. The economy with which he recreates the subtle variations in the whiteness of the snow by adding shadows in perfectly blended blues and pinks never ceases to be amazing. The subject itself is relatively unimportant. What counts is the realism that shows things accurately while at the same time bringing out their mysteriousness to best effect. A woman walking away down a road running between walls is used only to suggest that special silence that falls in winter when deep snow covers the ground in pure white. Sisley's landscapes touch us so deep-ly because we feel that, in each of them, the artist painted himself in painting what he saw. Like all the other great landscape painters such as Le Nain and Corot, Sisley always found the poetry that lies in ordinary things. As soon as he had settled in at Sèvres, Sisley got down to work and produced a number of views of the quayside, bridge and square of the town, as well as of the famous porcelain factory and a View of Sèvres showing the Bellevue road. The composition of these pictures is extremely sparing—a courtyard with an iron gate, a dusty road and a few rooftops rising above the trees were enough for Sisley to imbue this secluded corner of rural France with a unique charm.

During his years at Sèvres, Sisley never looked for unusual subjects or striking views. "The new," wrote Pissarro, "is found not in the subject itself but in the way it is rendered". As a result of recent research by Prof. Léopold Reidmeister, it has been possible to identify the exact locations of many of the paintings Sisley produced at Sèvres and, later on, at Saint-Mammès. Comparison of Sisley's paintings with photographs of the places they show provides fascinating insight into how much of Sisley's work is interpretation and how much is "true to life."

to me," he admitted much later to Arsène Alexandre, "that this tune, so gay, so musical and so enchanting has been a part of me since I heard it for the first time. It corresponds so closely to everything that I have always been. I sing it continually. I quote it as I work. It has never left me."

As well as music, Sisley found great comfort in his work itself. In spite of his poverty-ridden existence, he had the courage to go on alone with his work and to wait patiently for the success which, unfortunately, would come only after his death. Although a happy man by disposition, there were particularly difficult times at Marly-le-Roi during which he may well have believed that he had been forsaken by both God and man, and yet, even when it must have seemed that life was totally joyless, the joy he found in his painting remained with him always.

Sisley left Marly-le-Roi in the autumn of 1877 to set up house in Sèvres at 7 Avenue de Bellevue. The move did little to help him out of his financial difficulties, however. Only the friendship of the publisher Georges Charpentier, who never refused him a loan, saved him from clutches of his impatient

1   **Boat during Flooding, 1876. Canvas, 19³/4 × 24 in. Louvre, Paris.**

2   **Boat during Flooding, 1876. Canvas, 19³/4 × 24 in. Musée des Beaux-Arts, Rouen.**

3   **Flooding. Rue de Saint-Germain, 1876. Canvas, 18 × 24 in. Private collection, London.**

4   **Snow at Louveciennes, 1878. Canvas, 24 × 19³/4 in. Musée d'Orsay, Paris.**

1 Farmhouse Courtyard at Saint-Mammès, 1884. Canvas, 28³/4 × 36 in. Louvre, Paris.

2 Recent photograph of the "Farmhouse at Saint-Mammès," painted by Sisley.

3 The factory at Sèvres, 1879. Canvas, 23¹/2 × 28³/4 in. Private collection, New York.

4 View of Sèvres, 1879. Canvas, 18 × 15 in. Private collection, Paris.

creditors. He also received help from Eugène Murer, who had a cakes and pastry-making business and always welcomed his friends at his dining table. The painter and his family were invited almost every Wednesday to dine in Murer's restaurant in the Boulevard Voltaire in Paris. This was also a meeting place for Guillamin, the engraver Guérard, the novelist Champfleury, Renoir, Pissarro, André Gill, Cézanne and *père* Tanguy, the paint dealer. As well as feeding Sisley, Murer also found him work by ordering landscapes from him. Even more importantly, he busied himself in trying to sell his paintings and so helped him to make ends meet. On 3rd November 1877, for example, he organised a lottery in his restaurant in order to sell one of Sisley's paintings. Pissarro, Renoir, Guillaumin, Dr Paul Gachet and Sisley were all present at this "gathering."

Sisley's situation became increasingly precarious, however, notwithstanding the help he received from Georges Charpentier and Murer.

On 18th August 1878, Sisley wrote to Théodore Duret from Sèvres to ask for his help: "Might you be able to find some intelligent man among your acquaintances at the Saintonge who has enough faith in your artistic knowledge to be persuaded to spend a bit of money on a painting by an artist who is on the very verge of recognition? If you do know such a person, here is what I suggest you say to him: 500 fr. a month for six months in exchange for thirty paintings. When the six months are up, and given that he would never be prepared to keep thirty paintings by the same artist, he could try to sell twenty, thereby recuperating his original outlay and acquiring ten pictures free... As for me, I would be able to avoid spending a summer with no serious work to do, I could stop worrying and I might be able to get something good done." On receiving Sisley's letter, Duret found a buyer for seven of his paintings among his business acquaintances. This was Jourde,

1

the editor of *Siècle*.

In 1879, Sisley decided to present himself to the Salon in an attempt to get himself known and to open up new outlets for his work.

He wrote to his friend Théodore Duret on 14th April telling him what he intended to do. "I've been sitting here vegetating for far too long now—I'm tired of it. The time has come to make a decision. It's true that our exhibitions have been helpful in getting us known, and for that they *have* been useful, but I don't think anyone should stay in isolation for too long. We still have a long way to go before we can afford to ignore the prestige that official exhibitions can bestow. So I've decided to send some of my work to the Salon. If I'm accepted, and that may be possible this year, I think I might be able to sell something. To help me prepare myself for presentation at the Salon, I'm appealing to all those friends who have some interest in what I do." However, the jury of the Salon rejected Sisley's pictures, as was only to be expected. With this latest failure came other financial difficulties.

2

Having been evicted from his house in Bellevue, Sisley was obliged to find somewhere else to live, and since he needed money to pay for the move he was forced once again to write to Georges Charpentier for assistance. Charpentier sent money, and Sisley was able to rent a flat at 164 Grand'Rue in Sèvres. As soon as he had settled in, Sisley got down to work again and painted a number of views of the streets of Sèvres, including one of the famous porcelain factory. He also found new subjects in Meudon, Saint-Cloud and Suresnes.

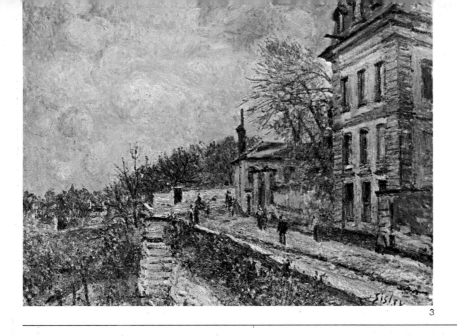

3

4

The painter of Moret-sur-Loing

Old Houses at Saint-Mammès. Autumn, 1880. Canvas, $19^3/4 \times 25^1/2$ in. Private collection, Paris.

"Moret is two hours from Paris, and there are plenty of houses to rent from 600 to 1000 fr. A market once a week, a very attractive church and some picturesque views. So, if you're thinking of coming down this way, why not call in and see for yourself? Veneux-Nadon is ten minutes from the station at Moret." Sisley's crisp, precise indications are contained in a letter of 31st August 1881 to Claude Monet, urging him to join him for a while on the banks of the Loing.

Sisley had already been there for a year and had immediately fallen in love with the peacefulness and rich greens of the countryside in the area where he was to remain for the rest of his life.

1

2

In June 1881, however, he made a brief excursion to the Isle of Wight. He wrote to Durand-Ruel on June 6th: "I've been for a few walks on the island, and as soon as my canvasses arrive I'll get down to work. The Isle of Wight is just as I imagined it, one big park, but I still think that people over-praise it. The place where I intend to work is right down at the bottom of the island, a superb area they call Alum Bay where many people go for walks. Ryde, where I am at the moment, is like any other fashionable English town i.e. it doesn't have much to recommend it from the painter's point of view. The favourite place for walks is the promenade; it's very long, as I know from continually walking along it over the past two days to where the Southampton ferry comes in, hoping to see my canvasses arrive at long last." However, due to the inefficiency of his suppliers, Bertrand & C., the canvasses never arrived and Sisley had to leave the island without painting even one picture.

Wishing to move nearer to Moret, Sisley rented a small house just outside the town, and almost on the edge of the forest of Fontainebleau in September 1882. As soon as he had settled in, he concerned himself yet again with trying to improve his precarious finances. He lunched with Monet in Paris on 14th November and the two men went on to visit Paul Durand-Ruel to talk to him about future Impressionist exhibitions. Monet insisted that "a personal exhibition now again can do more good for us than a joint exhibition" but Sisley wanted to organise new joint exhibitions. He wrote to Durand-Ruel on 5th November to repeat what he had said earlier: "All our experience tells us that joint exhibitions have almost always been successful, while with personal exhibitions the contrary has generally been the case ... now that we are no longer nomads and have a permanent, well-located venue to display our work in, I really think we shouldn't be trying to or organise new kinds of exhibitions or simply giving things a try to see if they work. In my view, our and your interest should be not so much to exhibit a lot of pictures, as to do everything we can to *sell* them. In order to achieve this, a joint exhibition with a few pictures by each artist would be much more effective and would have a better chance of being a success."

However, Monet's arguments proved more persuasive, and in spring 1883

3

1 Marie Bracquemond: On the Steamer, or The Pilot (Sisley and His Wife), 1882 ca. Canvas, 21¼ × 25½ in. Private collection, Paris.

2 Photograph of Alfred Sisley in 1882.

3 In a Boat at Veneux. A September Afternoon, 1882. Canvas, 18 × 21½ in. Private collection, New York.

Alfred Sisley seems to live again in this fine photograph in the Durand-Ruel Archives. Tall and thin, he looks more like a Scandinavian in build than a Latin. The grey jacket and large bow-tie are typical of the sober bourgeois dress of the period. Sisley believed in the dignity of his art and never affected a Bohemian way of life.

1 The Last Leaves of Autumn, 1883.
   Canvas, $28^3/4 \times 23^1/2$ in.
   Mr and Mrs Josef Rosensaft
   Collection, New York.

2 Letter from Sisley to Paul Durand-Ruel,
   Aux Sablons, November 1885.

3 The Loing and the Church of Moret,
   1888. Canvas, $21^1/4 \times 28^3/4$ in. Mr and Mrs
   David M. Heyman Collection, New York.

When, in 1885, Paul Durand-Ruel was in danger of being unjustly implicated in a scandal concerning fake paintings, Sisley immediately sprang to his defence and offered him all the support he could. 'Paul Durand-Ruel,' wrote his grandson Charles, "had denounced as a fake a painting supposedly by Daubigny, but Georges Petit, the owner, stated that he had bought it from the painter himself. In the face of this, Durand-Ruel withdrew his accusation, but several months later, inconfutable evidence came to light that the painting was, in fact, a fake and scandal ensued. Since Paul Durand-Ruel had publicly contradicted himself, his enemies saw their chance to question his competence as an art expert. It was obvious, however, that he was being pilloried by official and academic opinion for having embraced the Impressionist cause. Undeterred, Durand-Ruel published two courageous letters in Evenement that went beyond the narrow concerns of the scandal itself to show how he had, in the past, been one of the first to recognise the talent of artists like Millet, Delacroix, Corot, Rousseau and Courbet, and that he had been instrumental in establishing their reputations. Since the works of these painters were now rare, he was always looking among the young painters for artists who seemed destined to greatness." Shortly after the publication of these letters, Sisley wrote to Durand-Ruel warmly thanking him for having clarified the issue so well: "Dear M. Durand-Ruel, your two letters in Evenement are excellent. No one could have replied better than you have done, or have brought better to the attention of the public the silent war that has so long been waged against you because of your championship of our cause. Everyone is saying that you are right. It is a question not of commercial value but of artistic worth, a banner you have carried now for so long. For my own part, the things you say make me want to get down to work at once. Now is not the right time, however. It's cold, foggy, raining etc. We might have an Indian summer; if so, I can get started again. With kindest regards, A. Sisley."

3

Durand-Ruel organised a series of five personal exhibitions by Boudin, Monet, Renoir, Pissarro and Sisley in his gallery at 9 Boulevard de la Madeleine.

On 18th April, Sisley wrote a long letter to Dr Georges De Bellio about his wife, who was recovering from an illness, and he made use of the opportunity to talk about his work also: "We have had very good weather here. I have started work again. However, the spring has been rather dry this year; the fruit trees blossom one after the other but then quickly lose their flowers, so I have lots of work on the easel at the moment! The landscape painter's life is not always an easy one. The wind was so strong this morning that I just had to give up. It's clouding over now ... but not everything is sent to do us ill, as they say, because I am now able to chat to *you* for a while. Do you ever see Pissarro? Is he preparing for his exhibition? Is Renoir's going all right? I don't know when I'll have the pleasure of seeing you, and obviously, I have no news of my own for you."

Sisley's exhibition opened on 1st June 1883 with seventy wonderfully well-chosen paintings, but it was a complete failure. Four months later, in October, Sisley moved again, this time to Sablons, a quarter of an hour from Moret, where the climate was milder. He was immediately enthusiastic about the subjects he found to paint even just in his

Saint-Mammès, 1885.
Canvas, $21^{1}/_{4} \times 28^{3}/_{4}$ in.
Private collection,
New York.

1

2

own garden.

He wrote to Paul Durand-Ruel on 7th March 1884: "I'm back at work again and I've started a number of paintings (of the river banks)." These banks were those of the Loing which he never tired of painting, the banks of the Seine at Saint Mammès, the banks of the Celle and the castle of Croix-Blanche, the Loing dam and the barges of the port.

Several years later, in November 1889 to be exact, Sisley returned with his family to live in Moret-sur-Loing in the heart of the medieval town, first in Rue

de l'Eglise and then, in 1894, in a small villa with a walled garden on the corner of Rue du Château and Rue Montmartre, where he remained until his death five years later.

In February 1890, he was admitted as an honorary member to the exhibitions of the Société nationale des Beaux-Arts, which had been formed in opposition to the Société des Artistes Français and exhibited its work at Champ-de-Mars. This gave Sisley great satisfaction, and he wrote at once to the painter Alfred Roll to thank him for his help: "Dear M.

Roll, my friend Arsène Alexandre has written to me saying that it is thanks to your courageous intercession on my behalf that I was invited to take part in the National Exhibition as an honorary member of the Society. In past years I have always had to worry about how to get my work known, and in most cases my attempts have failed. You will appreciate, then, how sincere the thanks are that I owe you."

Sisley exhibited two oils and an acquaforte at the Seconde Exposition des Peintres Graveurs in Durand-Ruel's

1 **The Bridge at Moret and the Mills at Tan, photograph of 1882.**

2 **The Bridge and Mills at Moret, Summer, 1888. Canvas, 21$^{1}/_{4}$ × 28$^{3}/_{4}$ in. Belonging to Grégoire Salmanowitz, Geneva.**

3 **Photograph of the Sisley's house at Moret-sur-Loing. (Roger Viollet)**

4 **Road at Moret, Soft pencil drawing, 6$^{3}/_{4}$ × 6 in. Private collection, New York.**

Towards 1888, the town of Moret itself with its gateways, watchtowers, alleyways and snug roofs dominated by the church tower became Sisley's favourite subject. He often succeeded in conveying the contentedness of the town, seemingly asleep on the banks of the Loing, in the surface and depths of the river itself, the Provencher mill and the stone-arched bridge. At other times he painted the Matrat mills and warehouses, often of a November morning when the new light brought life to the winter landscape. No matter what point of view he chose, however, Sisley always placed magnificent skies over his water, mills and greenery. He was obsessed by the sky and did his utmost to render all its finest subtleties in all seasons and at all times of day.

3

4

gallery in Paris from 6th to 26th March 1890. The following month, from 15th to 30th May, he exhibited his work for the first time at the Société Nationale in Champs-de-Mars. His six landscapes, four of which belonged to the collectors Clapisson, Leclanché, Mallet and Montaignac were well received by the visitors to the salon.

Except in 1896 and 1897, Sisley exhibited groups of seven or eight of his paintings in Champ-de-Mars right up to his death.

During his years at Moret and in the countryside around the town, he produced a number of different series of paintings, sequences showing the same subject under different weather conditions or at different times of year.

The old houses of Saint-Mammès, the pathway to Sablons, the banks at Celle-sous-Moret or the meanderings of the poplar-lined Loing supplied Sisley with a whole repertoire of themes and subjects, even though the scene always remained basically the same. Towards 1888, one of Sisley's favourite subjects became the town of Moret itself with its gateways, watch towers and alleyways, and its snug houses sheltering under their old roofs dominated by the church tower.

In the final years of his life, from 1897 up to his death, he broadened his style somewhat as if trying to give the impression that he had won recognition at last, but what he gained in strength was lost in gracefulness and lucidity.

It should also be noted that even though it underwent a number of transformations, Sisley's vision always remained basically the same. While not wishing

57

to diminish Sisley's talent in any way, it can only be said that, in many of his *Banks of the River Loing* and in certain views of the edge of the forest of Fontainebleau, he seems to have lost the innocent suppleness of his earlier years. All too often, clumps of trees are rendered as gaudy masses of green, and their leaves seems lifeless, all the stranger since the effect is achieved with small, rather grainy dabs of paint which should actually *separate* the leaves, but do not in the context of the whole scene. The *impasto* of the houses cannot compensate for the uncertainty of their form, and his water has lost its earlier limpidity. We should be careful not to generalise, however. As Claude Roger-Maux says: "Even in the series painted at Moret, Saint-Mammès and Veneux-Nadon, we still often find the angelic tones of his earlier work. Insisting al-

1 **Rue de la Tannerie at Moret, 1892. Canvas, $21^{1}/_{2} \times 15$ in. Private collection, New York.**

2 **Rue de la Tannerie at Moret, 1892. Soft pencil drawing. Private collection, New York.**

3 **Moret-sur-Loing: the Bridge, the Church and the Mills, 1892. Canvas, $32 \times 25^{1}/_{2}$ in. Private collection, Paris.**

ways on what he affectionately called "the part of the painting the artist loves", Sisley makes the light shimmer in the leaves of pop-lars along a river or canal with the same gentleness of effect. Even when his hand seems to falter, his heart is not for that reason any less sincere." (*Preface de l'Exposition Alfred Sisley*, Galléry Durand-Ruel, Paris, 1957, pp. 7-8). We might add, finally, that what almost always redeems Sisley's weaker work is his wonderful ability to capture the light of the sky. In a letter to his friend Adolphe Tavernier, the art critic, Sisley gives a concise statement of the importance he always attached to the sky in his work: "Objects should be rendered with their own unique textures and, most importantly, they should be bathed in light as they are in nature. This is what we should be striving to achieve. The sky itself is the medium. The sky can never simply be a background. On the contrary, it serves not only to give a sense of depth with all its various planes (the sky has planes, just like the ground), but also to give a sense of movement with its form, its relationship to the general effect of the painting's

composition. What could be more wonderful, more full of movement than what we see in summer, the sky with beautiful white clouds scudding across it? What movement, what *speed*, don't you think? It has the same effect as waves when you are on the sea, exciting and fascinating at the same time. Then there is another kind of sky, later on in the evening. The clouds become longer and take on the shape of ships' wakes, like whirlpools that seem to stand immobile right in the centre of the heavens, and then gradually disappear, swallowed up by the setting sun. This is more tender, more melancholy in effect, it has the fascination of impermanent things, things that leave us. But I don't want to go on telling you about all the kinds of skies that painters love; I'll tell now only about the ones that I prefer most of all." With these brief notes and observations, Sisley helps us to understand why so many of his Moret landscapes affect us so deeply; the reason is that they convey to us, through the very way in which they are painted, the emotion the painter himself felt when he was present *in* the landscape.

Final years and death

The Loing Canal, 1892. Canvas, $28^{3}/4 \times 36$ in. Louvre, Paris.

Although he never moved from the region of Moret-sur-Loing during his final years, Sisley did make an excursion to Normandy in 1894, and he returned to England for the last time in the spring of 1897, two years before his death. It was thanks to the generosity of his patron François Depeaux, and industrialist from Rouen, that he was able, as he wished, to visit his native land for the last time. Since he had to go to London on business in any case, Depeaux invited Sisley to go with him and paid for a four-month stay in Britain, offering to buy in advance the two or three landscapes Sisley was intending to paint on the shores of the island. After a brief stay in London and a quick visit to the south, Sisley went to Penarth in Wales where he would find various subjects and seascapes along the cliffs of Langland. When he had settled in, he wrote to Gustave Geffroy to tell him his news: "I've been here for eight days after crossing southern England by train and stopping for three days at Falmouth in Cornwall. I'm now resting after this rather tiring journey before getting down to work again. The town is pretty, and the bay, with all the big ships sailing to and from Cardiff, is superb. I've read your two books; one is quite lovely, but *Enfermé* is an incomparably fine book. I read it from cover to cover in one sitting. I'm going to read it again more carefully now, putting it aside every now and again. It's the most interesting and moving book I've ever read. I don't know how long I'll stay in Penarth; physically speaking, I'm very happy here, in well-run lodgings with pleasant people around me. The climate is very mild, too hot even, especially as

1

1 **The Church of Moret, 1893. Soft pencil drawing, 12 × 9^1/2 in. Musée des Beaux-Arts, Rouen.**

2 **The Church of Moret in the Afternoon, 1893. Canvas, 32 × 25^1/2 in. Private collection, Lausanne.**

In addition to the series which convey the luminous poetry of the French countryside, special mention should be made of Sisley's fifteen or so views of the church of Moret which he produced between 1893 and 1894. Whether seen in summer or winter, in rain, sunshine or fog, in the morning or in the afternoon, with women going to the fountain to draw water or with birds circling round its tower, the ancient church is almost always rendered without perspective, rising solidly from the bottom of the canvas to fill very nearly three quarters of its area. Sisley's amazingly perceptive eye, as tasteful as it is geometrically accurate, positions both the transepts and the porch and towers of the façade in space with unerring perfection. Again, he captures the various times of year so realistically that each rendering of the church clearly reveals not just the season during which it was produced but even the exact time of day. Sisley's churches have often been likened to Monet's cathedrals of Rouen, and the similarity is no accident.

It is obvious that the two artists decided, each in his own way, to study the variations of light on the façades of old churches.

1

I write to you now. I hope to get something good out of what I see around me, and to return to my beloved Moret around October."

By November 1897, during his stay in Penarth, Sisley had painted several landscapes in Langland Bay and Cardiff Bay, and at Lady's Cove and Starr Rock.

On returning to Moret in November, Sisley decided to regularise his legal position by becoming a naturalised French citizen.

He had no idea how to go about it, however, so he wrote to his friend Adolphe Tavernier on 28th January 1898 to ask for help and advice: "My dear friend, I'd very much have liked to see you to talk about something that has been worrying me for some time. I want to take out French citizenship, but before I go about it I'll wait until it's a bit warmer because I'm suffering from very painful neuralgia at the moment. However, I'll waste no more time in telling you what I'd like to ask you to do for me. Since I don't really know how I should write to the Ministry of Justice about my application, I'm sending you a rough draft, and I'd be grateful if you could have a look at it and expand, change or correct it if you think it's wrong or badly put."

However, Sisley had mislaid a number of papers and documents during his various moves, so he was unable to act immediately on his desire to become a French citizen. Paradoxically enough, the English painter who, more than any other of the Impressionists, had had the skill needed to paint the landscapes of the Loing and the Seine, who was able to capture the "Angevin softness" the French poet Du Bellay wrote of, was to die an Englishman and not a Frenchman.

Faced as he was with these and other difficulties, Sisley lacked the strength to see through the many formalities in-

3

The art dealer Georges Petit organised a large-scale retrospective of Sisley's work in his gallery in 8 Rue de Sèze in February 1897, skilfully choosing 146 paintings and 6 pastels. Almost all Sisley's friends and collectors of his works were present at the opening, but the press remained hostile. Apart from a few articles by Arsène Alexandre and Adolphe Tavernier, the papers never even mentioned the exhibition, and Georges Petit was unable to sell even one of Sisley's pictures. For the artist, this failure was the final blow.

2

1   The Church of Moret, 1893. Canvas, $25^{1}/2 \times 36$ in. Musée des Beaux-Arts, Rouen.

2   The Church of Moret in a photograph of 1892.

3   Cover of the catalogue of Sisley's exhibition at the gallery of Georges Petit in Paris, 1897.

Studies by Sisley

1

During the summer of 1894, Sisley tore himself away from his refuge at Moret-sur-Loing to spend a few weeks in Rouen. At first he settled in the Hôtel du Dauphin et d'Espagne at 4 Place de la République, owned by Eugène Murer and his stepsister, who offered him a special discount. He then went to stay as the guest of the industrialist François Depeaux at his house at Mesnil-Esnard near Rouen. Sisley became a close friend of the shipping magnate from Normandy, and at his request produced a number of views of the meadows along the banks of the Seine and the farmhouses on the slopes of the Bouille.

1   A Barn in Normandy, 1894. Canvas, 19³/4 × 24 in. Private collection, Paris.

2   The Dining-Room of the Osborne Hotel in Langland Bay, 1897. Soft pencil drawing, 6¹/4 × 10 in. Dr. B. Jean Collection.

2

volved in naturalisation because he was now threatened by cancer, that most remorseless of diseases. He was also wearied by his constant struggle with poverty and his efforts to find ways of breaking down the complete indifference his work inspired in his contemporaries. Then Sisley's wife, his most faithful friend and ally during his career as a painter, died on 8th October 1898. Her early death was the final blow. Now alone, Sisley would end his life racked by physical and mental suffering. His letters to Dr Viau give us an account of the agony he suffered during the months leading to his death. Taking advantage of a relatively calm period in his life, Sisley wrote to the doctor on 28th November 1898 to give him his news: "I'm recovering better than I could ever have hoped from my latest haemor-

rhage. Although I'm ridiculously thin, my strength has now partly returned. I am undergoing local treatment with arsenic of soda: rinsing, washing, Pond's Extract powders, leg and back massage with Cologne water. I'd never have believed how something so simple could be so effective. So you see, my dear friend, I'm trying to pull myself round, so far as I am able."

However, a month later, on 31st December, Sisley wrote to Dr Viau desperately asking him for help: "I can't go on, my friend, I have no more strength left in me. It's all I can do now just to get into an armchair so that they can make my bed. I can't move my head any more because the glands in my neck, oesaphagus, throat and around my ears are swollen, and as things are now, I

don't think I can go on for much longer. However, if you know a doctor you trust who doesn't ask more than 100 or 200 fr. for a consultation, I'll see him. Tell me what time he's coming and I'll send a carriage down to the station. I offer you my hand in friendship, very affectionately but very sadly."

The following day, 1st January 1899, Sisley regretted having sent the letter and found the strength to send Dr Viau another message: "Take no notice whatever of the letter I sent you yesterday. I had an attack of the blue devils but I'm fine now. More than ever before, I understand the selfishness of animals: to have written to you on New Year's Eve of all times! Please forgive me, and accept my affectionate regards." Dr Viau rushed to Sisley's sick-bed in any case, bringing with him Dr Marie

of his work again, and it has rare breadth and beauty, especially one of the *Inondations*, which is a masterpiece."

This just assessment of Sisley's art by one of his peers was to be confirmed by posterity. By a cruel series of accidents and circumstances, the success denied Sisley during his lifetime came after his death. Only three months after he had been buried, the paintings left in his studio were auctioned to provide money for his children. On the day of the auction, art collectors and dealers were seen squabbling over his pictures. This sudden enthusiasm became fully apparent during the auction organised by the art critic Adolphe Tavernier on 6th March 1900. The *Flood at Port-Marly*, which

Sisley himself had been able to sell with difficulty for a mere 180 fr., went to Count Isaac de Camondo for 43,000 gold frances, and is now in the Louvre. Pissarro was right, and Sisley has now taken his rightful place among the glorious ranks of French landscape painters.

"Sisley," wrote Théodore Duret, "who suffered more than any other of the Impressionists, was, by some strange sort of compensation, the first to receive widespread public recognition." Early in 1911, the inhabitants of Moret opened a public subscription to erect a monument near the bridge of their town, and on 11th July, in the presence of the Undersecretary of State for the Fine

who prescribed his own treatment. But on 13th January the artist suffered another relapse. "I'm racked with pain," he wrote to Viau, "and by an anguished sense of weakness that I no longer have the energy to fight." Feeling his death to be near, he called for Claude Monet to say farewell to him and to entrust his children to his care.

A week later, on 29th January 1899, Sisley died in his house in Rue Montmartre in the shadow of the church he had depicted so many times in his paintings.

On 1st February, a cold grey day, he was buried in the small cemetery of Moret. Renoir, Cazin, Monet and Tavernier came down from Paris to pay their last respects. As they stood around the open grave, Cazin spoke a few moving words on behalf of the Société Nationale des Beaux-Arts as final farewell to the painter of Moret-sur-Loing.

Learning on 22nd January that his old friend Sisley was dying, Pissarro wrote these few words to his son Lucien, perhaps the most moving tribute of all to the English painter: "They tell me that Sisley is very ill. He is a truly great artist. I think he is as great as any painter that has lived. I've been looking at some

During his stay at Penarth, Sisley produced a number of broadly similar seascapes. Whether showing a rocky outcrop jutting into the sea, an enormous rock with foam-capped waves breaking against it, or bathers on a beach in a small cove, Sisley tried above all else to capture the way the light played on the sea and sand. The sulphurous yellow of the seaweed on the rocks is highlighted to bring out the transparent depths of the sea; the white sails of ships on the distant horizon are almost lost in the sky overhead. These Langland scenes, whose only elements—

the land, the sea and the sky—blend into wonderful symphonies of shimmering light to produce poetry of an indefinable magic, inevitably bring to mind Marcel Proust's descriptions of Elstir's paintings, in which he was perhaps thinking of Sisley's work: "The fascination of each of them lay in a kind of metamorphosis of the things they depicted, similar to what in poetry is called metaphor... These are moments when nature is seen, poetically, as it really is: this is what Elstir's paintings were made of."

3

Arts, Dujardin-Beaumetz, the local authorities unveiled Eugène Thirier's bronze bust of Sisley before the entire population of Moret, who had gathered together to honour the memory of the English artist who had lived, worked, struggled and suffered among them.

1 **The Roadstead of Cardiff, 1897. Soft pencil drawing, $6^1/2 \times 8$ in. Private collection, New York. (Photo by M.R. Schweitzer, Brenwasser)**

2 **The Roadsteads of Cardiff, 1897. Soft pencil drawing, $6^1/4 \times 10$ in. Musée du Petit-Palais, Paris.**

3 **Storr Rock, Lady's Cove Evening, 1897. Canvas, $25^1/2 \times 31^1/2$ in. Private collection, New York.**

Documentation

Sisley year by year

1865 Avenue of Chestnut Trees at La Celle-Saint-Cloud. Canvas, 19³/₄ × 25¹/₂ in. Ordrupgaardsamlingen, Copenhagen.

1867 Heron with Outstretched Wings. Canvas, 32 × 39¹/₂ in. Private collection, Paris.

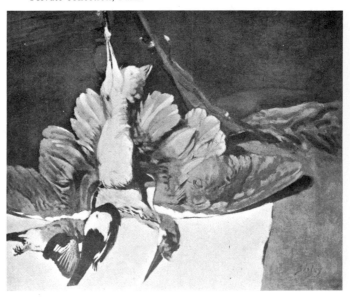

1866 Road at Marlotte. Canvas, 25¹/₂ × 36 in. Bridgestone Museum, Tokyo.

1868 On the Edge of the Forest of Fontainebleau. Canvas, 38 × 34 in. Mrs Joyce Ward Mackenzie Collection, New York.

1869
The House Among
the Trees. Oil on
wood, 3^{1}/$_{2}$ × 3 in.
M. Jean Chamoux
Collection, Paris.

1870
The Seine in Paris
and the bridge of
Grenelle. Canvas,
15 × 21^{1}/$_{2}$ in. Private collection,
London.

1871 First Snow at Louveciennes. Canvas, 21 × 28^{3}/$_{4}$ in. Courtesy of
the Museum of Fine Arts, Boston.

1872 The Isle of Loge Ferry, Flooding. Canvas, 18 × 24 in.
Ny Carlsberg Glyptoteck, Copenhagen.

1873 A Garden in Louveciennes. Canvas, 25^{1}/$_{2}$ × 18 in.
Private collection, Tokyo.

1874 Under the Bridge at Hampton Court. Canvas, 19³/4 × 30 in. Private collection, Winterthur. (Photo Dr H. Wolfer, Sulzer)

1876 The Market Square at Marly. Canvas, 19³/4 × 25¹/2 in. Kunsthalle, Mannheim.

1875 The Meadow. Canvas, 21¹/4 × 29¹/2 in. Alsa Mellon Bruce Collection, National Gallery of Art, Washington D.C.

1877 Boats Unloading at Billancourt. Canvas 18 × 15 in. Museum of Fine Arts, Belgrade.

1878 Le garage des hirondelles. Canvas, 17$^{1/2}$ × 25 in. Private collection, New York.

1880 Landscape near Moret. Canvas, 25$^{1/2}$ × 21$^{1/4}$ in. Private collection, New York.

1879 Winter Sunshine at Veneux-Nadon. Canvas, 19$^{3/4}$ × 25$^{1/2}$ in. Pacquement Collection, Paris.

1881 Orchard at By. Canvas, 21$^{1/4}$ × 28$^{3/4}$ in. Boymans-van Beuningen Museum, Rotterdam.

1882 Moret. The Boatyard at Matrat. Canvas, 15 × 21¹/₂ in. Private collection, Zurich.

1884 A Courtyard in Sablons. Canvas, 21¹/₄ × 28³/₄ in. Private collection, New York.

1883 Woman with Umbrella. Summer Scene. Canvas, 28³/₄ × 21¹/₄ in. Private collection, New York.

1885 Boatyard at Saint-Mammès. Canvas, 21¹/₂ × 28³/₄ in. Former Dr. Maurice Gilbert Collection, Paris. (Photo by Microfilmax S.A.)

1886 The Road from Veneux to Moret. A Spring Day.
Canvas, 24 × 28³/4 in. M.me Henri Goldet Collection, Paris.

1887 The Abandoned House. Canvas, 15 × 21¹/2 in. Private collection,
New York.

1888 Moret-sur-Loing. Canvas, 23¹/2 × 28³/4 in. Count Arnaldo
Doria Collection, Paris.

1889 Sunset at Moret-sur-Loing. Canvas, 21¹/4 × 28³/4 in.
Private collection, London.

1890 The Bridge at Moret and the Mills. Winter Scene. Canvas, $21^{1}/_{4} \times 25^{1}/_{2}$ in. Private collection, Paris.

1891 The Loing at Moret, Summer. Canvas, $29^{1}/_{2} \times 36$ in. Mr and Mrs Paul Haas Collection, New York.

1892 At Saint-Mammès. Canvas, $25^{1}/_{2} \times 36$ in. Private collection, Paris.

1893 The Church of Moret in the Sunshine. Canvas, $32 \times 25^{1}/_{2}$ in. Private collection, Winterthur.

1894 In Normandy. The Path along the River at Sahurs. Evening.
Canvas, 32 × 39¹/2 in. Musée des Beaux-Arts, Rouen.

1896 Boats at Berry on the Loing. Morning Scene. Canvas, 21¹/4 × 25¹/2
in. Mr Jacques O'Hana, O'Hana Gallery Ltd, London.

1895 Haystacks. Canvas, 23¹/2 × 28³/4 in. Andres E.T. Sperry Collection,
Buenos Aires.

1897 The Roadstead at Cardiff. Canvas, 21¹/4 × 25¹/2 in. Musée
des Beaux-Arts, Rheims.

Expertise

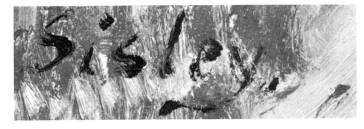

Three of Sisley's signatures.

Research by historians of modern art expert in the work of the Impressionists now enables us to identify the works of Alfred Sisley with great certainty. During his all too brief lifetime (he died at the age of only 59) Sisley produced some 900 oil paintings, 100 pastels and many other charcoal, coloured crayon and pencils drawings. In my *Catalogue raisonné* of 1959 I reproduced and analysed some 884 paintings produced between 1865 and 1897. Subsequently, I rediscovered about sixty landscapes whose history can be traced in full from the day they left their creator's studio. Throughout his life, Sisley sold or gave away his works to a relatively small circle of relations, friends, buyers and dealers. Thus, it is very difficult, if not impossible to come across an unknown Sisley nowadays. A work with no provenance i.e. one which was never owned by one of the early collectors of Sisley's work, one which was never mentioned in the files of his authorised dealers, or one which cannot be traced directly back to the studio of the artist himself is, in all probability, a fake.

However, painstaking research into the historical circumstances in which a work was produced, the production of a kind of perfect pedigree, can never be enough to authenticate a painting by Sisley. Before all else, the work—whether an oil, a pastel or a sketch— has to be studied in its own right.

Throughout this book I have drawn attention to the originality of Sisley's technique, and have tried to show how the great artist gradually developed a unique palette that enabled him to discover colour matchings that were both exactly right for his own purposes and original in their own right. It is this personal idiom that enables us to recognise a genuine Sisley at a glance. Artistic analysis thus becomes a sort of graphology—the stroke of a brush can be as revealing as the stroke of a pen or pencil.

Sisley almost always painted on standard *châssis* supplied by Legrand the paint dealer who was also one of his first admirers and supporters. He preferred light canvasses with a very fine grain. Apart from a few sketches, which he probably did not regard as finished works, Sisley signed all the pictures he sold or gave away, and he often dated them also.

Up until 1872, he wrote his initial before his surname, which had all its letters separated—"A. S i s l e y." Later, he became accustomed to signing paintings and pastels with only his surname in large characters using a brush and black, but sometimes also red or blue paint—"S i s l e y."

In spite of the difficulty of copying his unique idiom and style, an amazingly large number of fake Sisleys have been disco-

The Tug-Boat, fake.

The Tug-Boat, 1877. Canvas, 21¹/₂ × 29 in. Musée du Petit-Palais, Paris. (Photo by Otto Rheinlander)

vered. They can usually be recognised quite easily, and fall into three main groups.

The first and largest group includes "copies" of well known paintings that fakers have tried to pass off as originals. Often copied from colour reproductions, they generally repeat works belonging to museums or foundations. The famous *Tug-Boat* of Petit-Palais, which Sisley painted in 1883 on the banks of the Loing near Moret, has often been subjected to clumsy attempts at reproduction. Unfortunately, unscrupulous dealers try to pass off these fakes as variant works by the master himself.

The second group mainly includes unsigned landscapes, attractive studies by minor artists of the second half of the nineteenth century to which less-than-honest hands have added a fake signature. While these paintings rather overgenerously attributed to Sisley can easily be identified in most cases, it is often more difficult to distinguish Sisley's early works from those of his fellow students in Gleyre's Académie since Sisley and the others painted the same models at the same time under the guidance of the same teacher.

Finally, there is a third group of paintings that should never be confused with Sisley's own, although they do, quite legitimately, carry the name of Sisley. These are pastels and oils by Sisley's daughter which she often produced at her father's side during the years around 1895 when she was out painting with him. Naturally, the subjects tend to be the same. However, no matter which group a "fake" belongs to, a genuine Sisley can always be distinguished from imitations, and no fake can pass muster under rigorous expert examination.

Sometimes scientific techniques have to be used. Ultra-violet light, for example, reveals areas of the canvas that have been painted over, and can be useful in determining the authenticity of a signature. Chemical analysis can also be extremely useful because modern copiers use synthetic paints unknown in Sisley's time. In spite of all this scientific back-up, however, nothing can ever really replace the eye of an expert. The best way to expose fake Sisleys is to familiarise oneself with genuine works by haunting museums and private collections, to develop an extensive visual archive by committing to memory large numbers of his paintings, which then classify themselves spontaneously into "families," so that when we are puzzling over some newly discovered painting they come to the surface at the right moment and enable us either to accept the new painting as a member of the family or to reject it immediately.

Sisley's note-book (Carnet)

The great French collector Etienne Moreau-Nélaton owned a notebook of Sisley's drawings which he bequeathed to the Louvre on his death. For many years the existence of this notebook remained unknown to historians of the Impressionist period, and it was only in January 1959 that, in a short article in the *Gazette des Beaux-Arts*, Georges Wildenstein announced its existence and emphasised its extreme importance to scholars of Sisley's life and work.

For the first time ever, I reproduce here *in extenso* all sixty pages of this small, 12 × 19 cm, canvas-bound album which Sisley started in November 1883 and finished in the summer of 1885.

It is a *Livre de raison* (a sort of family diary kept by heads of families), a *catalogue raisonné* almost, in which the artist wished to preserve a record, in the form of rapid but significant sketches, of the paintings he was about to give away or sell.

In each drawing, Sisley wrote down not only the title of the painting and place it depicts, but also the size and shape of the canvas and often the name of the purchaser and the price paid. It is easy to see how important the Louvre notebook is, then, because it enables us to date about sixty of Sisley's pictures, identify the locations they depict and authenticate them with almost complete certainty. In the pages that follow, the finished pictures are often reproduced next to the sketches Sisley made from them.

4

5

Sisley's notebook was a kind of *Livre de raison* recording the paintings he sold or gave away. Some of the original paintings are shown from left to right and from top to bottom.

1 Between Moret and Saint-Mammès, 1883. Canvas, $19^3/4 \times 25^1/2$ in. A. Boissier Collection, New York.

2 The Loing at Saint-Mammès, 1883. Canvas, $15 \times 21^1/2$ in. Private collection, New York. (Photo Sam Salz)

3 Les Sablons, 1883. Canvas, $21^1/4 \times 28^3/4$ in. Private collection, New York. (Photo A. Frequin)

4 The Provencher Mill at Moret, 1883. Canvas, $21^1/4 \times 28^3/4$ in. Formervan Beuningen Collection. (Photo A. Frequin)

5 The Road from Moret to Saint-Mammès, 1883. Canvas, $19^3/4 \times 23^1/2$ in. Private collection, Manhasset L.I. (New York)

6 Old Barn at Saint-Mammès, 1883. Canvas, $21^1/4 \times 28^3/4$ in. Private collection.

6

Sisley's drawings are so exact that we can identify the landscapes he painted with almost complete certainty.

1 The Last Leaves of Autumn, 1883.
Canvas, 28³/₄ × 23¹/₂ in. Mr and Mrs Josef
Rosensaft collection, New York.

2 The Shingle at Saint-Mammès, 1884.
Canvas, 19³/₄ × 24 in.
City Art Museum, St. Louis.

Each drawing in Sisley's notebook is annotated in his own writing, thus enabling us to identify the landscape shown. Sisley often writes also the name of the buyer of his painting and the price paid. For example, six hundred francs (6 sans) to Georges Petit. From top to bottom:

3 The Croix-Blanche, Saint-Mammès, 1884. Canvas, 19³/₄ × 25¹/₂ in. Former Mellon Bruce Collection.

4 The Banks at Veneux seen from Saint-Mammès, 1884. Canvas, 21¹/₄ × 28³/₄ in. Private collection.

1

Sisley often gives the size of canvas after the title of the landscape. For example, "20 Canvas" or "10 canvas," meaning the standard canvas sizes he used. ($15 \times 21^{1}/2$ and $21^{2}/4 \times 28^{3}/4$ in.). From top to bottom:

1 A Road at Sablons, 1884. Canvas, $19^{3}/4 \times 24$ in. Private collection.

2 The Loing Canal at Moret, 1884. Canvas, $21^{1}/4 \times 28^{3}/4$ in. Art Gallery of Ontario, Toronto.

2

m top to bottom:

Saint-Mammès in the
Morning, 1884. Canvas,
15 × 21½ in. Private collection.

The Castle of Croix-Blanche
at Saint-Mammès, 1884
Canvas, 19¾ × 25½ in.
Private collection, New
York.

3

Sisley never forgot to sketch in the human figures that appeared in his paintings. His brief indications—a sort of painter's shorthand—contain all the information necessary to recognise the painting.

1 The Loing Canal, 1884. Canvas, 15¾ × 21½ in. Mr and Mrs Carrol S. Tyson Collection, Museum of Art, Philadelphia.

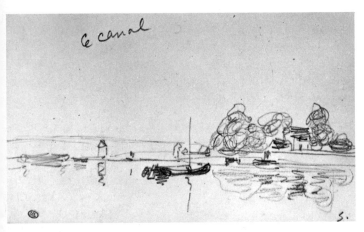

2

Typical Sisley landscapes. from top to bottom:

2 The Loing canal, 1884. Canvas, 15 × 21$^{1}/_{2}$ in. Private
collection, London.

3 The Loing at Saint-Mammès, 1884.
Canvas, 13 × 25$^{1}/_{2}$ in.
Mr and Mrs François L. Schwartz Collection, New
York.

3

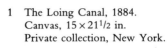

1 The Loing Canal, 1884.
  Canvas, 15 × 21½ in.
  Private collection, New York.

2 Morning on the Banks of the Loing, 1884.
  Canvas, 18 × 21½ in.
  Private collection, Paris.

The final sketches in the notebook reproduced here
show the landscapes painted during the summer of
1885. For example:

3 Saint-Mammès, 1885. Canvas, 21¼ × 28¾ in.
   Jack Lasdon Collection.

Books about Sisley

Few books have been written about Sisley's life and work.

The main source is François Daulte's *Catalogue Raisonné de l'oeuvre Peint d'Alfred Sisley* (Durand-Ruel, Lausanne, 1959). With a preface by Charles Durand-Ruel, the *Catalogue* lists 884 works, all reproduced and described, a critical study of Sisley's art, a detailed biography, a subject index and a list of who owns which Sisley works.

His engravings and lithographs have been catalogued by Loys Delteil in *La Peintre-graveur illustré, Camille Pissarro, Alfred Sisley, Auguste Renoir*, vol. XVII, Paris, 1923.

As regards his written output, Sisley has left us only his letters, and fortunately there are many of them. However, his complete correspondence has not yet been published. Extracts have appeared in the following books and periodicals:

Théodore Duret, *Quelques lettres de Manet et de Sisley*, in *La Revue Blanche*, 15th March, 1899, Paris; René Huyghe, *Lettres inédites de Sisley*, in *Formes*, November 1931, Paris; *Sisley*, in *Bulletin des Expositions*, Galerie d'Art Braun, Paris, 1933; Lionello Venturi, *Les Archives de l'Impressionnisme*, Durand-Ruel, Paris, New York, 1939, 2 vols.; Paul Gachet, *Lettres impressionnistes au Docteur Gachet et à Murer*, Bernard Grasset, Paris, 1957; Remus Niculescu, *Georges De Bellio, l'ami des Impressionnistes*, in *Paragone*, Florence, 1970.

In the last years of Sisley's life, or shortly after his death, many of his friends wrote about him in essays and articles which, together with his published and unpublished letters, are the main source of materials for Sisley's life and work. In chronological order, they are:

Adolphe Tavernier, *Sisley*, in *L'Art Français* no. VI, 18th March 1893, Paris; J. Leclercq, *Alfred Sisley*, in *Gazette des Beaux-Arts*, March 1899, Paris, pp. 227-238; Gustave Geffroy, *Sisley*, in *Les Cahiers d'Aujourd'hui*, Crès, Paris, 1923. In addition to the artist's own writings and those of his contemporaries, there are also the following monographs and books containing studies of Sisley:

Gustave Geffroy, *Sisley*, Crès, Paris, 1927; Georges Besson, *Sisley*, Braun, Paris, 1927; Pierre Francastel, *Monet, Sisley, Pissarro*, Skira, Geneva, 1943; Pierre du Colombier, *Sisley au Musée du Louvre*, Marion, Paris-Brussels, 1947; Gotthard Jedlicka, *Sisley*, Scherz, Bern, 1949; John Rewald, *The History of Impressionism*, The Museum of Modern Art, New York, 1961; François Daulte, *Les Paysages de Sisley*, La Bibliothèque des Arts, Lausanne, 1961; Leopold Reidmeister, *Auf den Spuren der Maler der Ile de France*, Propylaen Verlag, Berlin, 1963; Aaron Scharf, *Alfred Sisley*, The Masters Series, No. 24, London, 1966; Anna Maria Mura, *Alfred Sisley*, in *Maestri del Colore*, Milan, 1967.

SCHOOL OF
ART

STROUD

D

E

('ZS')